MY FAVOURITE PLACE

Edited by

Andrew Head

First published in Great Britain in 1998 by
POETRY NOW
1-2 Wainman Road, Woodston,
Peterborough, PE2 7BU
Telephone (01733) 230746
Fax (01733) 230751

Copyright Contributors 1998

HB ISBN 0 75430 456 6
SB ISBN 0 75430 457 4

FOREWORD

Although we are a nation of poetry writers we are accused of not reading poetry and not buying poetry books: after many years of listening to the incessant gripes of poetry publishers, I can only assume that the books they publish, in general, are books that most people do not want to read.

Poetry should not be obscure, introverted, and as cryptic as a crossword puzzle: it is the poet's duty to reach out and embrace the world.

The world owes the poet nothing and we should not be expected to dig and delve into a rambling discourse searching for some inner meaning.

The reason we write poetry (and almost all of us do) is because we want to communicate: an ideal; an idea; or a specific feeling.

Poetry is as essential in communication, as a letter; a radio; a telephone, and the main criteria for selecting the poems in this anthology is very simple: they communicate.

My Favourite Place is an exciting collection of poetry written by poets who have travelled far and wide, and the delightful experiences they have felt and seen are captured within this book.

The poems vary in style as they portray the moods and feelings of the poets' experiences.

This book is an adventurous collection of poetry and is a must for any poetry fanatic.

CONTENTS

AN AFTERNOON WITH JAMES GALWAY

Audience, atmosphere,
Assembly Hall,
bursting with electrical anticipation
as the first notes
transport us
heavenwards.

The music's sensitivity
sparkles, as does the man himself.
His eyes, his golden flute
and his black patent shoes twinkle
as he imperceptibly taps
the pulsating beat.

Flute and man are as one
when this genius performs.

The Londonderry Air, he claims,
is a musical prayer.
Indeed, I can almost feel God's breath
as I sit, holding mine,
spellbound.
His highest notes,
as clear as a mountain stream,
tumble, bubble,
then . . . are . . . still.
Tears well-up in ecstasy . . .
is this a foretaste
of my idea of Heaven?

Daphne Baker

FIREHILLS

Undulating, so elating, where green doth meet the blue
Sea that's so relentless, it's not as I once knew.
Crashing, bashing, smashing this land we want to save,
Eaten by the ebb and flow and swallowed by the wave.

Undulating, so elating, to walk across the green
Where once the Coastguard Cottage for many years had been.
Now gone to sea and gone to dust, beyond the rocky cave.
Coast eroded, signs foreboded, eaten by the wave.

Undulating, so elating, this land that saw my birth,
To walk up there, full joy and mirth, upon that springy turf.
Now the lashing and the thrashing of the sea and all its skills
Have worn away, another day, of life on gold firehills.

Undulating, so elating, the Firehills when alight
Above the surf, next green of turf, in gold and crimson bright.
Awesome sight, Nature's light, keeps up the hopeless fight,
Against the sea, that seems to be, that omnipotent might.

Nola McSweeney

BREEZES OVER THE GRAVESTONES

The wind blows over the gravestones
Of those who have gone before,
And gently whispers a lullaby
To those whom we see no more:
And it tells how the world has changed much
Since they lived and loved on this earth;
It tells of the wars and the conflicts they've missed,
And of building again, and rebirth.
So I join with the breeze as it lulls them to rest,
Whilst our lives hurry on at a pace;
I thank them for all they did in the past
To perpetuate this race.
For we are their 'tomorrows',
And with His helping hand,
Till we lie 'neath the sod, on our walk with God,
The grass will grow green in our land.

P M Spooner

THE GAIN

I can't forget
> the smells of India
> the beggar's hands in my face
> the closeness of people
> the colours of their gods
> the sadhus and the priests
> the nasal music everywhere
> the traffic and the cows
> the dhoti and the dhobi

the way nothing was wasted because of a great hunger for everything

I can't forget
> the ox-cart journeys under the stars
> the child so tiny on the palm of my hand
> the street vendors who met every need
> the loud and crowded press of it all
> the villages where they had never seen
> a white woman before

I can't forget
> how large and rich I felt
> and how they made me come home to such poverty.

Heather Freckleton

THE FENS

I came from the hills and valleys of Wales,
Which are shrouded in mists and rain
To the open vista and sun of the fens
To make a new home again
The spectacular spires so graceful and tall
Stand like beacons to show the way for us all
Around the bends some are so tight
It's hard to keep on the road at night
The churches, graveyards, windmills, and trees
Silhouettes in shadows on the light evening breeze

The tamed fields so fertile alive full of growth
Fields full of cauliflowers of which farmers can boast
Next it is cabbages flushed red what a sight
Then yellow daffodils, some pink and some white
Next year it may be linseed or rape
Or great brussel sprouts to put on your plate
May we continue to care for the land
And keep the balance between God and man

Jean Miller

RESPITE RIVER

Shimmering, rippling
Cloud reflecting
Smoothly flowing
Breeze deflecting
Leaf drops gathering
Wavelets slapping
      Clapping praise.

      And I praise too -
Quietly sitting
Peace absorbing
Beauty breathing
Soul restoring
Striving banished
Mind embalming
      Calming all.

Joy Tobler

MEMORIES OF MINE

To stand in silence near the place
where memories overpower time,
To feel the touch upon my face
of evening breezes passing by.

'Tis here I gave my answer to
a question asked so long ago,
Among the swaying branches through
which sunlight filtered onto snow.

My body trembled on that day
when tender words altered my life,
Soft lips that longingly did say,
'Please darling will you be my wife?'

And in this place I often stand,
Reliving joys of times long past,
But now I hold a loving hand . . .
A loving hand that's held steadfast.

Sue Brotherwood

A SENSE OF PLACE

I have only been here four years, in this country place,
Always I lived in the city, God changed that by His grace.
I love to walk the country lane, in spring the best of all,
When all things seem new, fresh and green.
The hedgerows, and the winter wheat,
The seat in town where I rest my feet,
A plough goes by my window here,
As through the glass my eyes do peer,
Muck-spreading to make things grow tall,
Ploughing, seeding, I see it all.
Yet most of all the harvest time,
With bales of hay, square or round,
Then the children try to climb, country life is so profound.
I love to sit and listen to the early birds,
I love to hear the church bells rung,
Some days, and Sunday morn,
It makes me glad that I've been born.
The smells of the country, pleasant some;
Chickens in the field,
After and before, the farmer comes to seed,
New lambs in the meadow, snowdrops, and daffodils.
O how I love this country town, it gives my heart a thrill,
I thank our God in Heaven, that He brought me here,
To live, to love, in this country town,
Of Walton-by-the-mere.

Constance Mary Martin

LONDON DUNGEON

London dungeon dark and dreary
Come inside it's really creepy,
Rats and blood, death and torture,
Mother dying cuddling daughter.

Some of it is horrifying,
Sound effects of people crying,
Moaning, groaning as they are dying,
Look around it's terrifying.

Christine Mountney

THE BLUEBELL WOODS

I walked the road that led me to
The hazy bluebell wood,
Anemone and orchid proud,
Beneath the hazel stood,
A carpet of a splendid blue,
Engulfed my eager eyes,
Such beauty I'd not seen before,
I gasped and then I sighed,
My ears, alert, were filled with song,
Of blackbird, thrush and wren,
I closed my eyes in disbelief,
And then, I looked again,
Each time I looked at beauty rare,
At nature's magic spells,
I prayed that time suspended me,
Within the blue, bluebells,
And for a while I too became
A shimmering, swaying flower,
Touched only by my sense of sight,
Spellbound by nature's power.

Lynne Elizabeth Hawkes

COUNTRY LORE

The image through the green blaze lies,
Reflects sensations from the skies,
Near earthen wise and shaded hand,
Gentle step on farrowed land.

Needled stab of blooded orb,
Makes festive present, in forest robe.
Urgent hunger, angry fear,
As stealthy flight is ever near.

Strident echo, warning call,
Through fingered stem and valley fall.
Imprints scroll in dewy cover,
Descends the deep to rippled river.

The vale breathes with woollen coat,
Call and answer, bleated throat.
Crook and hound, with careful view,
As pastel canvas is coloured new.

Kenn Evans

JACK FROST

Jack Frost runs between the trees
Leaving his icy trademark
Over fields he flies and swoops
Safe in the shadow of dark.

The lake lays soft and rippling
But as Jack creeps over it
A tender glaze follows him
Slowly bit by bit.

He moves onto his next victim
A lonely old path this time
He weaves between all the cracks
Until he hears the chimes.

The clock warns him his time is up
So Jack begins his retreat
He laughs at all this fun tonight
And knows he'll never be beat.

People complain when it is cold
But Jack knows they secretly love
The winter wonderland he creates
At night, like a silent dove.

Lindsey Brown

A FRONT LINE SOLDIER

A piercing sound, does frighten me
The whistling missile, no one can see
With beating heart, so loud I hear
The death drum thuds, with all I fear
I hug the ground, with scorching skin
Confusing brain, that lies within
A dense grey smoke, is all I see
These hidden men, are my enemy
With shaking hands, I grip with steel
The stumbling finger, the trigger I feel
I sight at scope, and open fire
These aimless shots, to field quagmire
Obey the order, I must move forth
Towards my adversaries, to the north
With bated breath, and tongue so dry
My will to 'survive' is my battle cry
I crawl to soldier, with twisted form
With missing limbs, and flesh that's torn
I hold his head, his glazed-like eyes
That slowly shut, this soldier who dies
A crack from cannon, awakes my sense
I now press forward, my feelings tense
And ground that shakes, from metal shot
Come flying smoulders, of shrapnel hot
I crouch and tense, and arms lock face
To God I pray, to my saving grace

T K Kennedy

BEAUTY

How can I describe, what does beauty mean
To me it is a picture that I ask my mind to screen
But, what to me looks beautiful, may to you look mean
So, how can I describe, just what does beauty mean

It may to you be strawberry, or something that is flowery
It could to me be snowberry, or some fine piece of shrubbery
You may just like it coloury, some ornamental chandlery
While I'd prefer the library and something that is literary

So how can I describe, just what does beauty mean?

How can I describe, what does beauty mean
To me it is a noise that I ask my mind to screen
But, what to me sounds beautiful, may just make you scream
So, how can I describe, just what does beauty mean

It may to you be heavy sound, or something with a brassy sound
It could to me be a fairground, yes something with a merry-go-round
You may just like it more profound, or some sound that will
me astound
While I'd prefer some ultrasound with you locked in the underground

So how can I describe, just what does beauty mean?

How can I describe, what does beauty mean
To me it is a feeling that I ask my mind to screen
But, what to me feels beautiful, may make you feel green
So, how can I describe, just what does beauty mean

It may to you be touching glass, an ornament in shiny brass
It could to me be velvet glove, or just the tenderness of love
You may, well like the feel of hay, or some lush grass where you
did stray
While I'd prefer some soft white snow that dissipates beneath my toes

So how can I describe, just what does beauty mean?

How can I describe, what does beauty mean
To me it is a taste that I ask my mind to screen
But, what to me tastes beautiful, you may find obscene
So, how can I describe, just what does beauty mean

It may to you be tasting wine, from some delightful Spanish vine
It could to me be spiced tomato, or just some darkest chocolate gateau
You may well like the taste of sweets, or some other forgotten treats
While I'd prefer some vegetable or something that is quenchable

So how can I describe, just what does beauty mean?
Through the senses of the owner beauty is serene

Paul Christie

BIRTHDAY

In a cafe
in Blackrock
an old jukebox
plays fifties' music,
bringing her back
to an innocent past
of ponytails
and bobbysox
and 'True Love Ways'
while the warmth
of his closeness
fills her nineties' day.

Anne Comerford

WONDER

I walked in bluebell woods today,
Heaven was very near,
The sweet sweet singing of the birds
Was music to my ears.
The fragrance of the bluebells,
The sun splashing through the trees,
The sight and sound of all these things
Brought me to my knees.

The tranquil peace that filled my heart,
Renewed me as I prayed.
I thanked my God for loving me
And this wondrous world He made.
He created it from darkness
And changed it into light,
He gave the birds and animals
To fill us with delight.
Their lives are intertwined with ours
In so many ways,
If we care and cherish them
God will bless our days.

Gwen Jones

HOLIDAY OF A LIFETIME

I awoke to the sounds of the doorbell,
closely followed by bangs on the door.
'I'm coming,' I yelled, 'hold your horses'
The banging just went on some more!

My best friend was there, in a fluster
and said 'Pack your case, it's no con.
I entered that comp in the paper,
for a holiday - guess what, I won.

My hubby can't come, he's commitments,
and I know yours is busy as well.
Perhaps we can swan-off together
to sand, sun and sea - ain't it swell?'

Well, my hubby agreed, and we travelled
to Spain, to the warm sands and sea.
I lay in the sun, then joined in the fun
till the gong rang and called us for tea.

The water was clear, sunshine speckled
we swam and giggled and splashed.
I felt like a kid (I know my friend did)
making sandcastles quite unabashed.

That fortnight the weather was gorgeous
and we both got a wonderful tan.
I sent Ken a card saying 'Miss you'
whilst Marie said the same to her man.

The time flew by so fast, it was eerie,
the two weeks just galloping by.
There we were, in the Malaga airport
and pretty soon we were high in the sky.

I looked down at Spain spread below me,
and it's sad that our holiday's done.
It's out with the pen and paper again
trying to win us another great one!

Jenny Smith

REFLECTIONS

The hills roll out before me
Wild flowers are all around
Oh! To be so carefree
And to hear the country sounds

The birds I love to listen to
As they proudly call their mate
Lambs frolic to and fro
They do not know their fate

Trees so old and yet so strong
Are reflected in a stream
That travels on a journey long
While I stand here and dream.

Doreen A Ogden

THE LONG WALK HOME

We reach the Heath at midnight,
The wind blows bitterly as we turn for home,
Turn into the wind,
This wind always feels like November,
But we follow the beacon of our thoughts,
Of a warm house and hot chocolate.
The Heath seems wider now,
And dangerous in a distant way,
'They buried dead people here',
Yet in the sunlight it is a happy place,
Darkness brings the shadows.
We walk in silence,
In awe of the darkness,
We listen to the night,
Listen for the voices of the dead.
We walk,
Resisting the urge to run,
To hurry away like guilty intruders,
Through the windswept silence.
We walk,
Until reality appears on either side,
And we leave the whispering shadows far behind.
But even when safe asleep in that warm house,
We cannot fully escape the darkness of the Heath,
The wind blows through our dreams,
Carrying with it the haunting silence,
And we shiver in our sleep.

Jenny Wright

THE LAKE

Pellucid lapping waters of the lake
Sweet zephyr sent to cool my fevered brow
Blest songbirds' music spilling from the bough
Warm summer's sun that soothes my sad heart's ache
Majestic mountains whence my hope I take
These favours bounteous Nature doth allow
Yet of these none compares with thee, I vow
For now my verdant soul thou dost awake
With fairer face than truth, and beauty's heir;
Till now from me my bitterness concealed
Thy faultless soul and ever-loving heart,
No mortal woman now, but goddess fair;
Inwit discerns thine inner-self revealed
And I begin to see thee as thou art.

Nicholas George Charnley

ALIEN WORLD

Diving down amidst warm sea currents,
so calm and still, urge to go deeper.
Little creatures dart around,
eyes transfixed by shimmering lights.

Darkness looms as depth increases,
there's abundant life, nothing ceases.
God's creation, a watery world,
a changing scene, now dark and cold.

Pressure building as depth increases,
need to rise, my mind's in pieces.
Regain my head as I slowly soar,
surface, that's the end of the mystery tour.

Rob Norcup

EAST WIND

Ballet of leaves in pirouette,
down the pathway dance.
Then, chase and chatter,
like noisy children,
up to the garden fence.

Quiet the choreographer, this east wind!

Old sycamore, stripped to the bone,
shivers in its wake.
Impassively, against the shed,
lolls a garden rake.

Orchestrates on high-wire,
sings bass, deep from chimney's throat.
Quite a versatile musician, too,
this east wind, and,
never drops a note.

Raymond K Evans

OCTOBER WALK

Gone the crisp step of summer,
The scene heavy and grey.
Decaying forest splendour,
Life is slipping away.

A soft dull clump
Through bare-boned trees.
An autumn rotting ground,
Floor thickened with leaves.

A startled cry and flap of wings,
This deathly place shades many things.
Seemingly so quiet at first sight,
This sleeping forest not dead, not quite.

A shift of shadow
Glimpsed through the trees,
The dripping and the dying
Hushed still by the breeze.

Return and see in six months hence,
The change in colour, mood and sense,
With the resonance of a summer's day,
And the lifting of the haunting grey.

Chris Thomas

BEING

I have escaped from the grinding rage of civilisation,
From the bonds and fetters of responsibility,
And sit now, here in the forest at the edge of the lake.
The air is warm and bathes my skin, gently, caressing tenderly.
The forest wraps my safely in its silence
And shares its mystery.

Here is peace as from the dawn of time,
Tangible stillness, calm clarity.
The only purpose of the trees is to be -
Just to be.

I listen to their message,
Knowing with the same instinct which makes the trees grow
That I can take this peace into my soul
Like seed corn, to be held in store,
Treasured and safely guarded in the vaults of memory,
A shield to be my protection
A magic talisman to keep my soul in tact.
When I return to the world
And face again its soul-rending choices
Its clamorous demands
Its false desires and empty promises
Then will I use the seed corn gathered here
In this place of peace.
Then will it bring calm and solace to my being
And remind me, that to be truly whole
I must just be.
Must still the jangling chatter of my mind
And just experience
Me.

Helen Brightstar

SNOW DOME

Surrounded by snow, in a world I've never known
a mist coats the ground, a chilling wind moans
I'm sitting in a snow dome
no way in and no way out
but, you know, I like it in here

Recycled plastic and metal placed on a mountain
I guess he had nothing better to do, accept creating
and so the rocks stopped falling
in the snow dome
it's beautiful my dear

A timeless location, where I'll never grow old
thinking about all the poignant stories I've been told
and all those feeling hearts that were sold
in the snow dome
everything is so sincere

Sounds of the natural symphony sing out
touching my inside, there's no-one else about
a tune so hypnotic, there's no doubt
that I'm in the snow dome
it's all so concise and so clear

How is it, I sit in cold, yet feel so warm?
My confused mind no longer forlorn
all those poisoned verses torn
in the snow dome
demons disappear

I wonder, will I ever feel like this at least once more
I can't remember ever feeling like this before
I'll stay a little longer on the snow covered floor
in my snow dome
where there's no ideas of fear

David Ares

ON BRIGHTON PIER

Wooden planks ring and rattle
With the feet and busy tattle
Of eager seekers for fun,
Onto Brighton Pier they come
Pushchairs with children running
Fathers cry 'Are you coming?'
Back and forth they surge
With that eager urge,
To be in on the joy
Felt by girl and boy,
Racing to the end of the pier
To see the sea if the clouds clear.
The pale sun shines through,
The music rises too.
Some sit and stare
Looking everywhere,
Friends are there to meet
With a kiss they greet.
Crying sharp-eyed white seagulls land
On old lampposts by 'Readers of the Hand'.
The sea changes from grey to green
And a faraway ship is now seen.

Shirley Patterson

LIVING NIGHT

A full moon hung in a still, cool night
The stars were absent, bleached by the light
The atmosphere made it an eerie night as
The glowing orb covered all with its light.
The cry of an owl was heard in the night as
A lazy mist crept along in the light.
This was the kingdom of living night
I couldn't but feel it, out there in that light.
The glow from the window a welcoming sight
Out there in the Kingdom of Living Night.

T E F Grimson

UNTOUCHABLE

My eyes creep inside of me
Full of energy unused
My heart begins to feel the emptiness
The place of vision becomes less and less

A resting body is all you can see
Inside I feel the pictures of water
I wet my hands and taste the laughter
Squeezing closer and running after

My body floating through the colours
Jumping feelings of places I've been
Reaching out to grab and hold them
But disappearing like the hope of all men

A voice in the distance
Invades and fades sense of thought
My eyes are wide as I look around
Man-made sounds as I place my feet back
On the ground.

Carly Henderson

WHEN AUTUMN FADES

As autumn's beauty fades away,
and winter starts to have her say;
though bleak may be, with skies so grey,
she too has beauty to portray.

For very soon the snowflakes fall;
they drape the trees, and cover all.
A feast to see, with fir trees tall,
in sheer amazement I recall.

The holly branch, with berries red,
enhance the scene, it can be said.
The robins gay, in search for bread,
and some of us make sure they're fed.

Vera Porter

CORFU CHURCH

Brilliant white stone building
Outside sanctuary olive oil,
Holy print glass-faced Madonna,
Black-dressed pilgrims.
Brown-faced tourists without religion,
Seek something
In new fresh flowers every day with olive oil jars,
Deep heat sunlight,
Sweat trickles down nose, on
Bella Vista Stella dusty road, and red-checked tablecloth.
Old women eat lunch,
Tourists drink beer,
Purple flowers shade,
Eternal life.
Small village life,
Young life lives on in deep purple groves,
And silver tomb of Spiros saint lies on,
In wooden icon reliquaries.
Quiet streets of old town, narrow cool,
Old square, new tourists.
Black hat priests, grey-haired and silver-crossed,
Religion in the streets,
And fly me home, develop pictures.

Christopher Owens

LOVE'S A BEACH

Soak up the sun
Like soaking up your love,
Changing the colour of my skin
Softening the hardness of my soul.

Listen to the waves
A constant crash upon the shore.
Like the assurances you give of a love
You dream of sharing.

Crystal clear the sunlight dancing on the water
Markers from the sand to the horizon,
Crystal clear the markers you have promised
In a future life together.

Watch us stumble in the shallows
Searching for a channel to something deeper.
Is our love so very different?
Sifting sand around a rock.

Appreciate diversity,
Hear the sea,
Feel the rock,
Soak up the sun,
Love's a beach.

Lisa S Williams

ARBOR LOW

Planning a picnic, the family of five
Sets off for the countryside; where should they drive?
Farewell to the city, its fetters and shrouds,
Follow the freedom of wayfaring clouds!

The lowlands forsaken, the village grows small,
As winding green hedgerow gives way to grey wall.
High, on a hillside broidered with sheep,
The monoliths lie in a ring feigning sleep;
The earthworks defenceless, the sentinels prone,
Absorbing the sun through their armour of stone.

No stir in the air, no sign from the mound
Of the magnetic forces at work in the ground,
As, drawn to a tryst by some unknown will,
The flock from the town joins the flock on the hill.
Inspection, intrusion - like many before
The visitors ponder the stones on the moor.

The lark in the heavens, the latchgate that creaks,
Both seem to question the silence that speaks.
A spring in the turf and a lift in the air,
A need overwhelming to prove what is there.
Off with the sandals - set the toes free,
'Come along little one, gambol with me!'

Silent, mid-circle, the seneschal lies,
Appraising the revels through lichen-grey eyes;
The table beside him windswept and bare,
Divested long-since of its sinister fare.
Passive, the giants doze on unoffended,
Evoking enchantment is what was intended.

The male-folk however, are caught unaware,
And stop in embarrassed amazement to stare
At the terrible sight of a mother gone wild,
Dancing barefooted along with the child -
The child who's forgotten that day in September;
I am the one who will always remember.

Audrey B Groome

PENDENNIS CASTLE

What ghostly hand ruffles my hair, I feel a tug, a stir.
The night is dark, yet gouged out with neon flash, the flickering
candles lit in lanterns ready for retreat.
Voices shrill and trill pleasantly, no cry of terror, but a drum
of strings.
This is a place of mists and seried stone in rounds.
Wet with the tears of exiles, bay of hounds.

Blood-red phantoms pace the bridge,
A horse moves to order

Gather round my
friends, one day
we'll know who
watches in the
mist.

V Jewell

MEDITATION ON A SUMMER EVENING

Beautiful balmy evening the heated sun gone down
We sat on the edge of the lake far far away from the town.
We'd come to be together away from the madding crowd
To join in heavenly silence far from streets and the traffic so loud.

Alone in this beautiful garden by the side of the dappled lake
With Nature all around us, spiritual love in us did awake.
As the circle drew silently closer three swans in the distance we spied
They'd come to join the circle for soon they were there by our side.

They joined us in sweet meditation for peace to reign on the Earth
To aid Mother Earth in her labours a Golden Age to give birth.
As we sat in quiet meditation bright stars in the sky shone above
Then Nature in all of her beauty enfolded us in heavenly love.

Marina King

EVENTIDE

I love the twilight, sitting in the gloaming,
When it's neither light nor dark,
A time of silence when no birds sing.
A time of peace between the night and day,
A time of rest and relaxation
When thoughts flow free in my imagination.
The cares of the day no longer exist,
All problems fade away.
As I listen to the silence no longer am I tense.
It's as though I'm in a dream, lacking thought or sense.
Where things are not what they really seem,
No people talking who insist
No tactical battles I must fight,
Just a lovely hazy mist as I wait for the night
In the sensuous stillness of the twilight.

Andrée J Saunders

A WALK WORTHWHILE

You couldn't see the hills that day
For mist had hidden them away.
But nonetheless a walk I took
'Twas either that - or read a book!
The dog was game so off I went
In spite of cold, discouragement!

Returning home I felt the cold,
Methought I must be getting old!
And wondered if I should instead
Have stayed within the house, and read.
But golden sunset brought a smile,
I knew my walk had been worthwhile!

R Baker

My Golden Afternoon

The sunlight glitters, dancing on the surface of the lake,
a bird dips, rises, leaving shattered sparklets in its wake.
The afternoon is hushed, as though the valley is asleep:
even the birds sing softly, this dreamlike state to keep.
The trees, full-clothed and flouncing,
spread their restless arms around,
shifting gently in the breeze,
with echoes of a sound
like taffetas and silks,
as if a rustling minuet
is danced amongst its branches to a tune it can't forget.

The lazy hum of bees becomes a soothing lullaby,
droning at me sleepily, tugging closed my eyes.
I feel the sunlight dapple, falling soft across my face.
Mosaic-like it twists and turns, exotic golden lace
a mere beauty of the moment
first vanishing - replaced,
patterning through shifting leaves,
each line and turn that's traced.
And I slip into a gentle dream,
dancing that ballroom tune;
quietly watched by a friendly sky on my golden afternoon.

Rosemarie Varndell

LOCAL BOOK OF CONDOLENCE SIGNING FOR DIANA, PRINCESS OF WALES

The queue's so long it stretches past the door.
In sombre patience, eyes fixed on the floor,
People whisper sometimes, raise their head.
Flowers held in tribute to the dead.
Men and women, children too are here;
A silent river flowing slow and clear.

For centuries our cathedral's watched the town
In splendid isolation, looking down
On those who never entered its stout walls,
But now the grieving population calls
As love for one they thought of as a friend
Brings crowds lamenting her so tragic end.

Tall arches, timeless chapels, shuffling feet,
All sign The Book, their pilgrimage complete.
Then back down the broad stone aisle,
In mood still grey,
And out into a bleak September day.

Joy Sanders

THE MAGIC OF THE FOREST

I walk in the sunshine through forest trees
Feel the warmth and the breath of the breeze
The rays are like fingers pointing at me
Lightning up my soul making me see
All the glories of the woodland glade
The leaves gather at my feet like a colourful
Carpet soft, blankets of moss mingling
Ready for nature to take her hand and colour them
Brown, red, yellow, and rust
Until they return back to earth - to dust
Forest glade where I roam - is this not a home
A haven for the discontented soul, to glory
In your beauty to wonder of your existence
Of your purpose I feel safe in your warmth
Like being back in the womb when time began.

Irene Rolland

DREAMS OF FLYING

Only at night, in dreams, can I
spread wide my arms, take off, and fly.
I'm freed from the Earth's gravity,
I can look down on house and tree,

can loop-the-loop in sunny sky,
flip over pylons, even try
to reach for space, where black holes lie,
where alien worlds wait for me.
Such a release . . . but I am free
only at night.

Will I feel like that, when I die?
No longer imprisoned in my
slow, heavy body, will I see
the universe? Infinity?
But until then, I'll sleep, and fly
only at night.

Laurel Wingfield

JILL'S QUESTION

Daddy where are we going?
Down the club little Jill's Dad replied.
But what club is that Daddy?
The Legion of course.

But what is the Legion Daddy?
The Royal British Legion if you please.
Yes Daddy but what is it?
It is for all who have served our country.
Where did you serve Daddy?
In war and peace my daughter.

But what are wars Daddy?
When one country does not like another.
But why don't they like each other Daddy?
They are people who want their own way.

But why is this wrong Daddy?
They are nasty and kill people.
Why do they kill people Daddy?
Because they refuse to obey.

Daddy let's hurry.
Why Jill where to?
Down to the Legion Daddy.
What do you think they can do?
Talk to the bad people Daddy.
Jill what will they ask them?
No more wars Daddy, only peace.

Dorothy Carter

THE LONELY VIGIL

It is now six months since you went
And still my emotions are not spent
I visited your grave today,
The sky, with snow, was leaden grey.

How quickly seasons come and go
Fields bare again, now white with snow
When we brought you there in May,
White flowers met us all the way
Six months gone with sun and tears,
The parting pain, like fire, still sears.

Was I the only one who cared,
Who took time out and came and stared?
Silently, I stood with you,
Taking in the shape and hue
Of that silent wintry scene,
Thinking, with joy, of all that had been.

And in the fading evening light
It seemed to me to be so right,
That on this anniversary day,
Where frozen soil met sky of grey,
That all the trees stood starkly bare -
But oh! how beautiful they were.

Then I knew, earth's cold could touch you not
You had become part of that quiet spot;
The grave had done its work
From this truth I could not shirk.

What will be . . . must,
Ashes to ashes, dust to dust.

Elizabeth Riches

FIELD OF STARS

Copper stills
Soaky hills,
Smoky cheeses
Atlantic breezes.

X's in words
Roosting of birds.
Clean streets
Rain sheets.

Bagpipes, harps.
Censers and grottoes
Cancioneros.

Apostles and viaducts
Alfonso, Jacobus
Pilgrims, Sant-yago
Hermits and crabs.

Seafood and granaries
Shells, pies, melodies
Sar and Sarela
Campo de Estrellas
The end of the earth
Galicia.

Steve Watkins

THE STATION

The station.
Crouched, waiting trainless by the railway line
Eyes foraging
A girl with grey boots
The undersides of yellow dustbins
Trees are staggered groping fingers, paralysed under the clouds
My vision is cluttered with bench seats
Shopping baskets, old ladies' legs, platform puddles
Noise of shuffling, chattering, distant cars
An aeroplane.
People assembled in dishevelled formations
Ten 'O' clock in November
Still waiting for a train.

Stuart Shafran

LONDON LIVERPOOL STREET

'Tickets please' at two minutes
Buildings searching for community
Brick walls hail me to my left
Not stopping at Stratford.
Look at that river -
Tunnel negates photosynthesis
- It's a stream anyway.
Why Ilford depot? Is
Pylon town really Bethnal Green?
Clouds disilluminate clarity
Of Chadwell Heath, where
You barter for three thoughts
Per stop. But now,
'This is Romford' and
Another church sighs.

Michelle Brown

STONEHENGE

Psychedelic wardrobe pilgrims,
Sacred tor gathered.
Round tower eyes diluted
In the
Lemon zester sun.

Rainbow bus commune,
Set out on a Salisbury plain.
Bluestone, sarson and stone lintel circled.
Standing on the axis of a translucent lozenge.
That is a midsummer sunrise.

Paul Dunne

LAKE LOUISE - JEWEL OF THE ROCKIES

I fell in love Louise, right from the start
First time I saw you I didn't want to part
It was in summer and you looked your very best
A jewel in the clouds way out in the west.

Your home is the scenic Banff National Park
I've been smitten for years, you've sure made your mark
Named after royalty, the magic is in your beauty
To tell the whole world I feel is my duty.

Marilyn Monroe and Arthur Miller heard of your lore
Their honeymoon took place in the hotel by your shore
In the 1950's that was, long ago to be sure
Before I knew of your water, so green and so pure.

Forever adorning postcards as well as educational books
You're loved by folks for your stunning good looks
I shall see you again, that I do know
It will be in summer, not when there's snow.

I fell in love Louise, right from the start
First time I saw you I didn't want to part
It was in summer and you looked your very best   .
A jewel in the clouds way out in the west.

Gordon M Graham

THE DREAM

I laid me down beside a stream and had what seemed to be a dream;
I heard a voice say 'Come with me and see the things that ought to be.'
He took me gently by the hand and far we travelled over land,
Over seas and mountains high, until it seemed we reached the sky
And there such peace did dwell that how I felt was hard to tell.

The folk all lived in harmony, without fear or deep anxiety
A smile on each and every face, a warm hello, a kind embrace.
Front doors were left open wide, no fear of evil going inside,
Instead a welcome on the mat, a 'Come inside and have a chat.'
No fear for children out at play, no need to watch in case they stray;
They all looked after one another, Father, Mother, Sister, Brother.

If only all of us could see, that this is how it ought to be.
Instead we'll just go on our way, destroying each other day by day;
Raping and killing for lust untold, not caring what age; be
                              they young or old;
Robbing and cheating to satisfy greed; no mercy will show,
                              no conscience to heed.
Polluting the air, the water and land, to make our lives easy,
                              a little more grand.
We don't seem to grasp that all we are doing, is killing
                              the things we think we're pursuing!

Audrey Sollitt

RUBBISH TO TREASURE

The early morning mist still gathers as car booters arrive at the gate,
Best pitches are allocated one-by-one with the furthest spot to the late.

Refreshments vans start the fried onion smells that waft
                                        across the stalls,
People are busy arranging their wares before the first
                                        of the customer calls.

People drift in from their Sunday lie-in and amble from
                                        one boot to the rest,
One man's rubbish, another man's treasure as folks
                                        clutch buys to their chest.

From handbags thru' tools and records to food the
                                        choice of purchase is wide,
Some haggle the price whilst others don't buy 'cos
                                        it's just a day out for a ride.

Midday draws near and the booters pack up as custom
                                        starts to drift and dies,
The early start was worth the money tins jangling
                                        and visitors celebrating their buys.

Jackie Hale

IN GOOD HANDS

I ride the white ceiling until,
silent and still,
my wheeled-in bed
is surrounded
by clinical air. Wafting in
pre-med calm, Yin
and Yang at bay,
I wince. 'You may
feel this.' I hear too late. My hand
now prickles, and
I feign reply
'. . . two . . . three .. . four . . . fi-'

Tony Harris

SWIMMING FOR SERENITY

Stepping into the water's embrace,
Cool and inviting not missing a place,
Floating weightless, a sensation so calm,
A feeling of safety away from all harm.

Maybe a far off memory from before birth,
Or being one with nature, a part of the earth,
Twisting and turning within its restraint,
Sounds soothing, sleepy and faint.

Light flickering through the surface above,
Glittering like jewels given to someone you love,
All of these emotions and more, make me want to be,
In this comforting place of peace and serenity.

Kevin Dent

BUS TRUCK

In the warm breeze of a Flores night comes the truck
With its cargo of human kind
Nestled in the back
On cosy wooden benches

Grandma climbs up with a live chicken in her hand
Everybody seated to the clucking sound
Biscuits and bananas so sweet to the taste
And a sharing that is sweet to the heart

Off into the night over bumps
The bones inside our bodies shaken
Teeth like rattles clanking
No gentle suspension to cushion our buttocks.

Helen Wadley

ELEPHANT FIELDS

In the silent grey vastness of Elephant fields
Even the flowing reeds in the far off distance are still
Nobody knows us, nobody cares
Everybody ignores us, but everyone stares
In the silent grey emptiness of Elephant fields
Nobody except me carries their heart on a shield
Life is something we're all trying to live
Love is a feeling we all try to give
Sometimes I feel so wooden with no real heart
It bleeds so badly all the time we're apart
But still nobody knows us in these Elephant fields
It's a phantom of the past running alone at full tilt
So why do I love thee in so many ways
The weeks, the years, those elephant days
Will we ever meet again in life's Elephant fields
If the time ever comes my heart would be still
Let the memories bring back the long gone dead
Some who we miss, others live on in our heads
The ghosts of our pasts still feel the chill
Of the ones that we lost in those Elephant fields.

Richard Hoskins

THE DESERTED HOUSE

The crumbling mansion stood,
In the hot summer noon,
Crowding closely, the wood,
Threatens to engulf it soon.

Padlock rusty on the hasp,
Broken windows blindly stare
Ivy clings with a firm grasp,
The demon decay is there.

On broken hinge, the gate,
Hangs among the grass,
The paths are overgrown,
Since no footsteps pass.

Through the greenhouse roof,
Tendrils of an old grapevine,
Fruitless - as in proof,
Of the years of decline.

Quietly leave this dying place,
That once had tender care.
Though I cannot see their face
I feel there's someone there.

Frank Cooper

ON A DIFFERENT DAY

... that day as the warm evening air
caressed my brow, I strolled quietly
through the park and my mind
floated free of the weight of anxiety.
I felt unusually close to myself,
and enjoyed it, for now I'd escaped
the pressure of yesterday; and you
could postpone tomorrow, for it had
no part to play in how I felt that day ...

Kevan Beach

WORLDS APART

Viewed, from another world,
Though cosmic years apart,
Focused on a glorious sphere,
The image clear and sharp.

Marvel at vast oceans deep
In awe scan mountain peaks
Embrace like children snow-bound lands,
And hot dry desert sweeps.

Zoom in on forests jewelled with dew,
Roam fields of golden corn,
Enchanted spy majestic falls
Amid green valley's lawn.

Be-mazed by colour a rainbow no less,
A prism of sky, land and sea.
Oh! It's sad to think the glories beheld
Was once a description of thee.

Alas, those scene's haunt every dream,
Console not! Your now, ugly mass,
A petrified orb cloaked in venomous mist,
No trace of one's former sweet past

Yet, just beyond the southern band,
There's hope we've fixed our sights,
Upon this world resembling you
When heaven bore no greater delights.

Carol Fay Clarke

I REMEMBER D DAY

On that great day of June the sixth, in nineteen forty four,
I rose before the break of dawn, felt drawn towards the shore.

I felt excitement in the air, the mist had eerie feel,
As if it was the dawn of time, I felt an urge to kneel.

I knelt and prayed for freedom, an end to this long war,
Then when I raised my eyes aloft, a miracle I saw.

Through swirling mists like angels' wings, as far as I could see,
Were rows and rows of Allied ships, all heading straight for me.

I raced inland to spread the news, they're coming, it's today,
The Allied troops will land at dawn, our freedom's on its way.

Wave after wave they poured ashore, passed by to fight inland,
Though many fell and gave their lives, lay dead on foreign sand.

Fifty long years have now gone by, since that immortal day,
When in the mist of that June morn, I knelt alone to pray.

To all who fought upon that day, we owe our freedom now,
The future will remember them, in freedom this we vow.

If on that day you were not born, or were too young to go,
However can you realise, however can you know.

How felt each man to be a part, of that armada brave,
Each laying his life on the line, a foreign soil to save.

Show to all of those brave men, they suffered not in vain,
Just guard and cherish freedom still, ensure it will remain.

The way you live and work and play, may not be to their plan,
But for your right to make the choice, they risked all to a man.

Alan Terry

HOMESICK

In this landscape of sky
and villages hidden by flatness,
I feel so vulnerable, so alone.
I miss the deep sided valleys,
the dry-stone walls that embrace them,
waterfalls shouting from gullies,
the limitation of horizons.

Here, I can see for hours
across the stark fields
that lie in wait for next years crop.
The armchair in this cottage
fits like a stranger's overcoat
and even the warmth that dances from the fire
does nothing to stop this chill I feel.

Ray Pilling

THE VISION

With inward vision
I climb the winding road
that leads to Beachy Head
and reaching level ground
see the undulating Downs
stretching far as I can see.

And in my dream I see
high-summer of my
childhood days when,
grass once green was
carpeted with blue round-headed
rampion and scabious nodding
in the breeze
and in the distance,
far below the tall white cliffs,
the sun makes silver ripples
on the sea.

Pamela Korn

THE HOSPITAL VISIT

Row upon row of white shrouded metal tubular beds,
All are occupied apart from one
Why is it empty?
What has become of him?
Windows that remain closed
Closed off from the world.
Little swarms of dust motes
Glisten and dance
In the sun's rays.
Balloons of red and white
Rhythmically drop their fluid
Down from one
Down from one,
Filtering through the tubes
Gradually feeding sustenance
To the open veins,
Absorbing greedily
The red and white jewels of life.
Toxins flow away, stored, packaged . . . discarded.
Sleep, sleep, suspension, suspended.
Bleep, bleep, breathe so deep
Deep, deep, deep
Is this sleep?

Michelle D James

WALKING IN SUNSHINE

Walking in sunshine
My Lord is there,
All my griefs he helps me bear.

As rain clouds gather,
With a heavy heart
My weary way I begin to start.

The glistening pavement,
A sparkling jewel,
Takes away all that is cruel.

A bending willow
Graceful and green,
Memories of beautiful scenes.

Times gone by,
Baggy Point with its Ling,
Butterflies abound as I sing.

Walks with my father
In wellie boots clad,
Thick with mud and a little mad.

He taught me the song birds
And others beside,
I cried and cried when he died.

We walked beside rivers
And the Devon moors,
I loved those dramatic craggy tors.

Walking in sunshine
My Lord is here,
He takes away every tear.

Jennifer Hedges

ALEXANDRA PALACE
'ALLY PALLY'

Remembered days of youth long past
of happy days spent playing round
that noble building, time went fast,
so many pastimes to be found.
The views of London stretching out
distant river catching the light,
turn the head and look about
so much to see from up that height.
Shouts from the race track just ahead,
the sound of bikes not far away,
acres of grass on which to tread
and precious, endless hours to play.
Sometimes going roller skating
(fun if you could stay upright!)
Hear the organ while you were waiting
to hire some boots that weren't too tight!
Car sales, boating, even a fair,
never bored, there was too much to do,
climbing the trees just for a dare,
winter, sledging 'til soaked right through.
Memories I have to treasure
fun to recall when feeling down,
remembered times that gave me pleasure
the jewel in life's glittering crown.

Joiann

QUIET ROOM

Spirits in their glory
Telling a ghostly story
A thousand distant voices heard
Yet not a word, not a word.

Ne'er a jest or joke
Or laugh in spiralled smoke
What secrets could be told
From vanished canvas old.

No pattering on the quarried floor
Or squeaking from the large oak door
Flickering shadows from the windows tall
Tantalise spiders on the limestone wall.

Silently breathing the embers burn
Remnants of wood, in the blackened urn
While numerous insects silently creep
To keep this room in unmolested sleep.

N F Letts

SEA FRET

The sea fret grips ev'rywhere
with cold clammy fingers
as perspiration, the dead.
The body is red loam
lying beneath its thick shroud
of swirling grey sea mist.
High tide draws it to the coast,
the sea is its birth place
a cauldron that is the womb
and to the end sustains.
It will dictate each movement
that it decides to make.
Even controlling the ebb
while the waters recede.

Fernley Sing

AN APRIL EVENING

The sun shone through the boughs of the trees
Her hair slightly moved with the cool April breeze
Her heart did wander to the one she loved most
The man in her dreams, the one she holds close.

Her sleek young shoulders and rich dark hair
Is nature the beauty, or dare I compare.
Her eyes hold a secret, too painful to mention
Is serving this man, a hard loved lesson?

The evening is young and the sun still warm
And this little lost girl prays for the love she has sworn
Through the trees he comes, she smiles so sweet
Soon he'll be holding her close, their love complete.

They stroll through the fields leaving reality behind
Their hearts for each other and loving on their minds
The time that they have is so precious and near
And the sun silently goes and in her eyes is fear.

She knows so well the next path he'll take
Is the kiss and the wave, as he slips through the gate
Once again she stands there, all lost and alone
As the love for this man is a seed that has grown.

P A Deakin

THE BEGGAR

The blind beggar sat at the end of the street
With a begging bowl that lay at his feet
Odd times he would hear a clink in the bowl
And call out his thanks to some passing kind soul.

Some people passing he knew them by name
For no two human voices are exactly the same
Some were very young and some were much older
And some carried the weight of the world on their shoulder.

Some were dressed poorly, others wore furs
Some had a conscience that couldn't be stirred
Some people were generous and some were unkind
One was heard to remark, 'Is he really blind?'

Some gave a penny and some gave a pound
Some missed the bowl and it fell on the ground
Some stayed to chat and some walked on by
Some felt so sad that they wanted to cry.

He could guess their emotions, he was fully aware
As he gazed back at them with a sightless stare
Thinking don't pity me! I accept what I've got
It's long ago now since I accepted my lot.

Long ago I dreamt it would be lovely to see
But the gift of sight was not destined to be
However you see I am a man of great wealth
For God in his wisdom gave me my health.

Ray Spoors

SMELL OF FRESH AIR

I sit and smell the breath of fresh air
Often captured by the pollution around
The wind crawls upon my face so fare
No people, no noise, the world actually looks round.

I imagine laying in between a million flowers
Smelling the scent like I've never before
I sit await watching the passing hours
Wishing these days would come much more.

The leaves on the trees wave from here to there
As I close my eyes and drift off at sea
I fix my eyes, I gaze and stare
Can it really, really be me?

Sleeping now in a bed of daffodils
Only me in my own world isolated
Across the mountains and up the hills
My own world I created.

I open my eyes and look everywhere
I feel not like I did before
I look around with not a care
I wish these days would come much more.

Afshan Novrin

ON MY WAY HOME

I'm on my way home
From a day at the beach
With a smile on my face and a bite at my peach.
Two men and a woman at a bus stop are standing,
Outside the strange religious building.
They've been drinking and arguing.
A fist in the face, a knee in the crotch.
The woman protects the non violent aggressor.
Punches are flying, the fat man going crazy,
The woman falls to the ground and is kicked in the face.

I look on, it's quarter past five,
I'm safe in my car, I'm on my way home.
The traffic is building up behind me
What can I do?
I want to help, my neck twisted back
Observing this obscene
I'm moving slowly, time has changed.

Decision, decision
Bumper to bumper
Foot to face.

The fat man notices me
He walks away self-consciously.
Slowly leaving the bus stop
Becoming aware of the traffic stopped
Watching his display.
The woman is holding her face
The small man is comforting her.
The fat man meandering away.
I'm on my way home.

Derek Young

DUSK

Patches of light fade over an amber sky,
As daytime slowly drifts away,
Blackbirds sing in sweet harmony,
Giving thanks for a wonderful day.

Dewy drops settle on dried out grass,
The cows take a late evening munch,
Whilst rustling leaves settle down to sleep,
As the lights go on, one by one.

Glassy yellow eyes prowl the hedgerows,
Winged bats dart madly here and there,
An eerie silence swamps the soul,
Broken only by a distant hooting owl.

Seen through changing greyish hues,
Tree branches stand, stark and still,
Whilst wildlife scurry to their secret dens,
As darkness shrouds this busy world.

Diana Frewin

THE SNIPER

Yonder, all beyond him dies
as under quiet moon he lies.
A stranger, here, yet brought to pass
rows of victims, in which tall grass,
whose wormy stench assigned to doom
hold poignancies of ghostly gloom.

Will it be his to wander free
away from shade of forest tree;
hear again the Peewit crying,
leave the pain, decay - the dying
here does he see the fields of home
here, find peace where the birds have flown?

'Walk up,' quick on trigger to score,
labyrinth dark where sun is no more
shoot behind cover nimble prey
as darts and twists elusive way.
Link flesh with flesh, like fallen leaf,
or poppy fresh whose dust is grief.

In groping years that follow on,
most of 'Immortal Band' are gone.
They the few that are still alive
hold, in their power to survive
a hallowed living whole, who see
'Deserts of Vast Eternity'.

Kathleen Ross

THE HARVEST OF LOVE

The gentle rain is softening down,
A timeless benediction
Caressing Earth in her summer gown
While birds are clear of diction

The blossom fades and floats away
As new leaves meet the skies
Enfolded in a greener way
While birds proclaim their cries

The days grow short
While leaves are caught
And gently torn asunder
From trees lit up with wonder

And now full circle
Wends the year
Entwined in a wheatsheaf girdle
And garlanded with bitter myrrh
The seasons tell of God's concern
Which sends us rain and snow
To blanket Earth and keep her warm
Preparing for the new growth

The myrrh was given to the Babe
To symbolise His dying
Upon a Cross His Life He gave
To end our quest and striving

And now the seasons show His love
In mixing pain and pleasure
He leads us as a gentle Dove
His blessing in full measure

While God's rich fauna is supplied
God's bounty is for all men
Whose needs will never be denied
When Jesus' reign begins again

Valerie M Smith

THE SUN BROKE THROUGH

Things looked dismal
What a pain!
While it was cloudy
With so much rain . . .

Days of grey . . .
Kept coming our way . . .

It was distressing
And needless to say
Quite depressing . . .

Then one day
The clouds blew away.
The sky turned blue . . .
At last . . .
The sun broke through . . .

Carol

THE LEGEND OF CAMELOT

Camelot, rich imagination of mystery and power,
King Arthur, Merlin, the magic sword of Excalibur,
Fair maiden Guinevere, Arthur's queen,
A beloved wife, but faithful not,
Knights of the Round Table, and heroic Sir Lancelot.
Wonderful places, in these stories of old,
To bring dreams of romance with knights gallant and bold.
A sad tale of forbidden love affair, to hurt King's pride,
Story set in rugged English countryside.
Passionate love affair, between Guinevere and Lancelot,
Bringing trouble to enchanted castle at Camelot.
This love triangle, happy and sad, thrived in the golden mist,
But Mordred, evil knight, put end to this.
Guinevere to burn at stake, to save King's face,
Sir Lancelot rescues her,
But now they have to leave enchanted place.
After bloodshed, tears, sad fall for all,
Enchanted land torn apart that day,
Sad music on a mandolin does play,
For broken holy law,
The price, they had to pay.

Julia Holliday

BERLIN 1976

Down the East German 'corridor' a long lonely trip
Empty and desolate no people, no animals, no life
I am so tired yet I feel I am watched, I dare not stop.
Mile after mile no movement no sound, even the birds
Fear to fly in the overcast sky which pours down
Endless sheets of cold damp drizzle
There in the distance, movement and life, my heart lifts,
Is the nightmare over? No! It has just begun, barriers,
Barbed wire and tall grey towers. Fear loosens my
Bowels as soldiers on tanks turn cruel eyes down the
Barrels of their guns. I'm just a tourist, what on earth
Have I done?

I pass through the barriers and think I've gone mad,
London, Paris, New York all wrapped into one.
Thousands of people, hundreds of languages, a melting
Pot of cultures oh! I want to laugh, cry, jump for joy,
What a feeling. I have never been so excited, so happy
I let the feeling lift me, everyone is my friend, a whole
City with a never ending carnival. Night turns into day
And the party goes on and on . . .

The further I moved away from the city centre the more
The euphoria left me, the colour and life slowly began
To fade, I looked up to see the towers and the fences
Looming over the city and I realised that on this oasis,
Fenced in by mines, guns and barbed wire. Trapped and
Isolated in the middle of the land of the 'enemy'. There
Was no rescue, there would be no help. If those heart
Stopping sirens sounded, for these people and me it
Would be the end.

I left the city the next day and never returned.

Donald Tudor

THE PIAZZA

We sit together my friend and I,
beneath the sun in a flawless blue sky,
lazily sipping our gin and tonics,
watching the famous Italian histrionics.
A commotion reaches us through the air
as a frustrated mother screams in despair
when her children escape her and run wildly around,
one falling head long on the grimy ground.

A young Casanova preens himself in the glass
while watching and waiting for young girls to pass.
Two other young men have cornered their prey
with well practised charm to convince her to stay.
Lovers stroll by caressing and kissing,
not caring for the sights they are missing.
A dog is sleeping in the afternoon sun,
children are playing and having fun.

The smell of fresh coffee wafts under our noses,
young gypsy girls wander around selling roses.
The water in the fountain sparkles in the sun
mesmerising both of us as we watch it run.
Tourists are wandering around with their maps,
the ones tired and weary are taking naps.

In the restaurants nearby people are eating,
colleagues, families and friends are all meeting,
chattering and laughing, savouring their food,
everyone enjoying this holiday mood.
This image will stay when it's time to go home
sustaining us both till the next time we roam.

Jean Adams Perryman

MARCH 1997

Wow what a spectacular sight.
I've seen the comet Hale Bopp tonight
A wondrous shining ball, so bright,
With a tail, long and burning white.

And what's that, just to the right,
That constellation, clear and bright
Another lovely sight to see
Cassiopeia, a W Shape, to you and me.

Wow, look south, and look at Mars
A bright red planet, hanging among the stars
What a lovely sight,
Adding even more wonder to the night.

Oh look up high over head, and you can see
The familiar Plough, shining down on you and me
What a marvellous sight is here,
And visible throughout the year.

And yet the biggest, and the best
Of constellations, is in the west
With Rigel as its brightest star
Is Orion, so near and yet so far.

Oh look, Sirius is close by,
Like a beautiful jewel in the night sky
Shining bright, and shining blue,
Twinkling and sparkling, with such a lovely hue.

These are all out tonight
Shining in the sky, so clear and bright.
And as we look, and as we stare,
Praise God who has made, and put them there.

Carolyn Brook

A GLIMPSE OF HEAVEN

The end of a weary day draws to its close,
And as upon my bed I lie in sweet repose,
I gaze into the star-spangled night,
Hoping the vision I have seen with delight
Will return.
The dream that has enchanted me before,
And I will whisper, please encore,
For in the daylight hours, my vision fades
Into some far corner of my mind,
And I am left without recall
Through the many hours that fall.
Perhaps in some quiet moment,
At sunrise, or in some high place,
The vision will return, and I will be enchanted.
As with open eyes I perceive the beauty, of that aura,
I will rejoice again.
And there upon that summer morn,
A most wondrous sight to see was borne,
Thrust upon the dazzling scene,
A vision, transcending all that I have ever seen,
Perhaps 'tis a glimpse of heaven that I see
And I am overjoyed.

Hubert Hayes

HEAVEN IN MY GARDEN

Deep amongst the cabbage patch,
The runner beans and peas.

No one there to talk to,
No one else to please.

I love to wander round my land,
Just soaking up the sight.

Breath the scent of wallflowers,
Admire lupins with delight.

I feed the birds and watch them play,
Basking in the sun.

The trees swaying gently in the breeze,
I'm with nature one to one.

It's so peaceful here it's heaven,
I can think of nothing else to match.

Wandering round the garden,
Deep amongst the cabbage patch.

Caroline Perry

LAST GIG

Walking on stage, instruments in hand,
The crowd cheers in a deafening roar;
Smiles on their faces, they proudly stand,
This is their last gig on their last tour.

The music begins ever so gentle,
Rising in volume with graceful poise;
A cacophony ensues from this mantle,
Meshing together, forming white noise.

Consumed by the heat of the moment,
I'm blown away by the rhythmic beat;
The atmosphere's an electric current,
Dodging around the stomping feet.

The band announce their very last song,
Cheers from the crowd build up to a chant;
Everyone joins in with the shouting throng,
I try to resist but find that I can't.

All is now quiet, the lights come on,
Exhausted smiles are all that's in sight;
Etched in my memory from now on
Are the emotions I felt here on this night.

Gavin Watkins

THE DREAM I DREAM

I walked along the beach again
The weather changing from sun to rain
I watched as the drops fell into the sea
The wind whipping up, my hair blowing free.

As I sat upon the sandy shore
I wondered what my life was for
The waves on the sea would glisten and gleam
And I'd sit for hours and live my dream.

I looked to see the orange glow
Of the setting sun descending so low
Then it appeared, the silhouette
A vision of which I would never forget.

A man on a horse came into sight
A handsome man on a horse of white
He rode along the edge of the sea
Until he neared, he'd come for me.

He kissed my lips, how sweet the taste
On his horse we rode, my arms round his waist
Together we stayed under the moon above
The cool wind soothing the warmth of our love.

Then I'd return to my life so cold
With no one there to love and hold
Without the man whom I long for so much
The hero of whom I will never touch.

B Malcolm

FOOTPRINTS

Footprints were there . . . In the sand so deep
       Someone ahead was just out of reach
Walking alone . . . A need to feel free
       As I was that morning . . . Down by the sea.

Wind was keen like never before
       Waves were rough hitting the shore
But the footprints ahead were large and deep
       So far spaced that I had to leap
Each foot I placed in that sculptured print
       Carried me nearer and I began to think
But the footprints had gone with the flow of tide
       No one in sight . . . Nowhere to hide
Bubble had broken . . . Gone from my world
       Like a mirage . . . A Dream . . . Not a trace to be found.

Gwen Tominey

COMPLACENCY

Sitting here at the grimy station,
Waiting for a train.
The heavens decide to open,
I'm getting thoroughly drenched *again*.

Mind ticking over,
Collecting all my thoughts.
Hardly remember what it was,
The reason why we fought.

Trudging to the drinks machine,
Praying for a hot cup.
Bashing and banging . . .
Damn thing's packed up.

Loud slow tocking,
Of the dated station clock.
My train pulls up to the platform,
Coughing and wheezing as it stops.

I see you running down the platform,
Hands in air.
Begging my forgiveness,
People stop to stare.

The argument patched up,
Still pouring . . . road home long.
I really must learn,
That *sometimes* I can be *wrong*.

Tracy Bell

LOURDES

Living with a disability;
It's not much fun in the beginning
As times goes on though
It becomes part of your everyday life.

Lourdes, it's cheerful but peaceful
It's the place to see
The place known to cure people and
It's the place that's done it for me.

It may not have cured my physically
But it has mentally
It's being in the presence of this unique atmosphere
That works wonders even if you don't know or see it.

There's one thing I've learned from this special place
Live life to the full and
Don't let people discriminate you 'cause
Life's too short and
No disability can stop you doing what you want (to do).

Lourdes, it's definitely a place to see
Whether you've got a disability or not
It's a place you can find peace and
Never feel out of place
Lourdes, the place I'll never forget . . .

Denise O'Donnell (18)

SPRINGTIME

I walk along the bridle path, sun shining overhead,
Hoping in my heart that gloomy winter has fled.
Breaking through at last are patches of blue sky,
Amid the bands of white clouds sailing way up high.

Bare branches are busily budding again,
Their delicate tracery decorating the lane.
Blossom sprinkled on hedges like powdered snow,
Whilst on the pussy-willow catkins grow.

In gentle breezes daffodils nod their heads
Hyacinths and tulips adorn the flower beds.
Speckle-breasted thrushes sing a sweet song
Carrying food to their young all the day long.

I look across the fields to see rabbits playing there,
With pleasure I halt my walk to stand still and stare.
It's great to be alive on a day such as this,
The simple pleasures of life I do not want to miss.

Christine Naylor

BATHED IN BLUE

I listen
To this living, vibrant unknown place.
It feels like there's nothing
Between me and the world.
But no wind touches my face,
No shadows vary the darkness.
Then I open my eyes
And I'm surprised
To be
Bathed in blue.

Underwater,
Yet able to breathe.
Deep,
Deep blue,
All around.
Sounds
But no images.
Only blue
Surrounds
And supports me.
Nestled
At one
With myself.

Linda Breeze

In Wales

How *awesome* are the mountains,
Standing majestic and tall.
With heather and bracken of various hues,
- And here stand I - so small.
Fast running streams, and beautiful lakes
A range of colours no artist can pen.
Quietness and peace just seem to exude
From the hilltop, down through the glen.
Content to roam the hillside
The wildlife just roam free
Unafraid of human presence,
At peace they also seem to be.
The running water, pure and clear,
As it down the mountain pours,
Shines and glistens in the sunlight,
Reaches the waterfall - and roars.
High up in the hillside,
Quietness reigns supreme,
Flowers swaying in the breeze
By a gentle running stream.
Rabbits playing in the meadow,
And the sheep just graze nearby.
A blackbird in a hawthorn bush
Watches us, as we pass by.
All so very beautiful, and different
Could anyone ask for more?
There, waiting for us to enjoy,
The Britain we adore.

June Bootle

TRAFALGAR SQUARE

There is a place
I long to be
Trafalgar Square
Is the one for me.

The big dark lions
Sit big and proud
Touched by millions
From north to south

The chatter of people
Feeding the birds
The clicking of cameras
As the tourists emerge.

The sound of a hooter
As the traffic rolls on
A sight seeing bus
With lots of people on.

Men and women rushing
With no time to spare
Many Nationalities
From countries here and there.

Different coloured taxis
Old fashioned buses too
It's chaotic but I love it
It's London, through and through.

Denise Hemingway

SUMMER'S DAY

A silent summer's day has come,
So full of health and strength,
No more the cold to make us numb.

Tranquillity reaches us on long drawn out days,
The sound of insects buzzing all around,
Fields smell so sweet and rich as you sit and laze.

Each new dawn of a summer's day shimmers
                            through your open window,
The choir of birds in harmony they sing,
Smells of fresh cut grass drift over from the meadow.

The trickle of your garden stream, for you it's calling,
Rays of sun reach down and reflect upon your soul,
No longer do you feel as if you are falling.

Life is everywhere, buzzing bees collect from flowers,
Frogs and fish leap through the warming waters,
Horses graze in the paddock, forgotten are all those city towers.

Rebecca Simmonds

TAKE HIM DOWN

'Take him down,' he says,
In a voice harsh and loud.
Down to the cells I am led,
Away from my love and the crowd.

I see my love weeping,
It tears my heart apart.
Into the 'sweat-box' I go,
And to the jail, depart.

All is light, but dark.
My world is in colour, but bland.
I feel trapped in a nightmare:
A perverse Alice in Wonderland.

Every night I pray before God,
That when I wake up I'll find,
That I have returned to home,
And left this hellish place behind.

S B Dyer

AVEBURY

The white horse glistens
and the evening's dawn
tracks the flight of birds
over magnetic fields of exile

In cradled silence the infinite
crushed by gravity's groan
as the dancing bones
of breath in light attest
the I is other than is known

Near the water's edge
fission fuses into second sight
scorching the outer darkness
freeing the waters of life.

Luke Hopkins

SNOWSTORM

Crystals of ice gently fall
        upon my reddened face
with coldness that yields to
        their beauty and their grace . . .

Exposed skin raw where
        the harsh wind touches
sends flurries of snowflakes
        as the cold wind rushes . . .

A pure white blanket covers
        as far as the eye can see
on the horizon in contrast
        dark silhouettes of trees . . .

Stand tall with bark bare
        naked in the night
as snowflakes land to clothe them
        in gowns of pure white.

Alison Blackburn

THE PLACE OF MY CHILDHOOD

Looking about, I find the whole place strange,
It's as if things have gone through a change.
There's the lane much narrower than I recall,
Those fir trees I knew them when they were small.
Looking at the lines of sheep wire, you'd never guess,
There used to be hedges where birds did once rest.

Grey drab walls, the farm-yard surround,
Muddy pebbles and stones tramped into the ground.
Broken window panes mended with tape,
White-wash discoloured, in a run-down state.
Overlooking the fields where I spent my childhood days,
The river Lagan is still making its way,
Through the rocks that I used to climb,
They seemed so much bigger in my childhood time.

The sheep all nibble around,
For the tufts of grass that can be found.
What has happened to the place of my childhood dreams,
Where the fields were rich and covered with green.
It seems to have aged without grace,
This barren land has taken its place.

Silence now fills the air with dismay,
Where once children's laughter did stray.
I get the feeling that if this place could cry,
Nowhere would there be found a dry eye.
For like the tree I once swung from,
The place of my childhood memories is gone.

Pauline Uprichard

SAD SENSE OF BEING WHERE THEY'RE HOMELESS

How does he live and fathom life
Within the bitter cold wind disturbed nights?
Did he ever live a childhood of fun and play?
What brought him here
To the lonely streets to stray?
To make his bed;
On the dusty streets he lays his head.

Has he always been this way?
Or did he once rise
With determination of prospects
And life with family ties.

Did he pull himself up
From the slums once before
Determined of this life,
He could gain so much more.
Believing he could have the things
We all ignore?

Like a wall and a ceiling
Behind a locked wooden door.
Toast in the morning
And porridge for a treat.
Tea in a tea-cup,
And soft kitchen seats.

Richard Turland

THE FAIR

There are shouts in the air,
As we enter the fair -
That exciting and magical land,
Where the swingboats go high,
And in clouds seem to fly.
Oh, it's thrilling; it's glorious, it's grand!

On the roundabouts gay,
We forever could stay,
And enjoy the fun of the fair.
Have a coconut shy!
You can't fail if you try.
Here you'll feel that you haven't a care.

Have a go at Aunt Sal,
Can't you hit the old gal?
Oh, come try, try again and you will.
Take your chance everywhere;
Join the fun of the fair.
With elation and joy your heart fill.

Eileen N Blackmore

LOST AND FOUND

Close your eyes and weep no more
picture the shore.
Golden sand,
hear the birds,
a vision that will never die.

Close your eyes to see your home
sailing
through the thundering waves
roaring blue dragon.
Hold tight to your memories.

Close your eyes, let go
the pain.
Imagine my warmth, my arms.
I see and feel
and watch, but I tell you, it's not your time.

Open your eyes, see the land
the birds that fly,
hear the voices
sirens
they'll take care of you now, goodbye.

Ruth Goodall

AN AFTERNOON AT ST PETER'S CHURCHYARD

It was a lovely clear day and I could see for miles
At a place where people come to visit and go away with smiles
As I sat on a seat in the churchyard of St Peter's Church,
Boughton Monchelsea, admiring the wonderful view of God's
Countryside at its best alive and peaceful too.
I felt it was the perfect place of peace and quiet to speak to God
And pray as I was filled with a wonderful feeling that he wasn't
far away.
Yes I felt so very close to God there that it was easy to understand
Just why God had His house built here on such a delightful piece
Of land. The Church is very beautiful and one that God will always
treasure as He listens to the worship that takes place in there which
gives Him so much pleasure.

Royston Davies

FLYING FASCINATION

Arriving to embraces, smiles and cheers,
Departing from heartaches, sadness and tears.
All shapes and sizes coming and going,
All colours and creeds to-ing and fro-ing.
Tiled floors, clicking heels,
Pushchairs, trolleys, luggage on wheels.
Colours, textures, robes of all nations,
Forgotten passports, panic stations!
Where has he come from? Where is she going?
Goes away pale, comes back glowing.
To Australia for good? A fortnight in Spain?
Up north for a meeting then straight back again?
Remembered the tickets? The camera? The cash?
Tablets for sickness? Cream for a rash?
Check in the luggage, a quick bite to eat,
For take-off and landing, best suck a sweet.
Language unrecognised, what are they saying?
Visiting Britain? Where are you staying?
Hide in the lavatory, don't want to fly,
Deep breaths, keep calm, try not to cry.
Tannoy announcement, time you got going,
Down to gate twenty and onto a Boeing.
Find your seat and get strapped in,
Engines whining, what a din.
Unbelievable power, beyond understanding,
Thousands of tonnes taking off and then landing.
It gives me goose bumps down my spine,
The roar of the engines and that high-pitched whine.
Says a voice, 'Are you not travelling my dear?'
'Oh no, I'm just here for the atmosphere!'

Sandra Lewis

THIS DAY EVERLASTING

This day everlasting, new-born, yet old -
My spirit is reaching for something untold.
My body finds field, my lungs the spring air
And yet I'm longing for something *out there.*

So warm is this day, so golden, serene,
I soak up its beauty but seek the unseen.
My mind searches archives of memories past,
For walks and the friendships I wanted to last . . .

So many flowers out, bird songs and buds -
They promise me heaven as my feet touch the mud.
I wonder on days as strange as this one
If the race I run is nearly over and done.
Well, what is death? - When spirit leaves bone -
Just pure, secured rest in a brand new home.

Joanna Riches

LOVE IN PARADISE

Aroha, Love O come with me
To isles of sun and mystery;
Where swaying palms dance to and fro,
While moon-tipped waves with phosphorous glow.
Across the golden sands we will walk
In peace, there is no need for talk;
The songs of bird cling to the air,
They carole out their joy, to share.
I will take you swimming in a pool,
The water's deep and crystal cool;
Young people come to nature's prize.
To view it all with lover's eyes.
But when at even, stars appear,
By firelight gleam, I will hold you near;
Until at last in sweet content,
Red dawn awakes, and night is spent.

Cynthia Beaumont

BLUEBELL WOOD AT BROCKWEIR

Delicate, trembling shades of blue
Blending to a distant view,
Lapping round the silver trees
With green-leaved spears all sparkling
                in the breeze.
A million bluebells carpeting the ground -
What better sight in springtime to be found?

Honey-scented,
Well presented,
Bluebells standing calm and still,
A picture, painted on a sloping hill.
And then, a sudden breeze across the
                coloured ground,
What shimmering pleasures can there
                be found!

Eileen M Lodge

READ ANY GOOD BOOKS LATELY?

Every citizen can use their public library
Young and old - rich or poor - every colour or creed,
Local council's provide this vital service
Where we - the public can sit, or - take home, a book to read.

Here - in the library - one can find tranquillity and quiet
Away - from the constant traffic roar, out there, in the street,
Where the staff are helpful, knowledgeable, and well-read
For to answer, all the public's questions - is no mean feat.

And the books? Love stories abound, in almost every novel
Plus - some envy - greed and hatred - to boot,
Even murder - and mayhem - corrupt and double-dealings
Reliably - your librarian - will find you, a book to suit.

From photography to politics - from gardening to 'The Raj'
Even the most discerning - can find a book to read,
In the world of cookery - the culinary art
You may find something new and 'yummy' - on which to feed.

From yachting to the stage - from fishing to World Wars
Every single subject - has a story to relate,
Most books are written - by the top people in their field
Their expertise - is given to us - 'on a plate'.

From Britain to Calcutta - from China to Peru
In your favourite armchair - you stay home, and enjoy a world tour,
Jet-lag? Malaria? Seasickness? Lost travellers' cheques?
These are the trials - you won't - have to endure.

When there is 'rubbish on the telly' and your video is 'on the blink'
Oh dear - tonight - you are really 'in shtook'
But - despair not - your foresight will prevent a frustrating evening
Remember - yesterday - you borrowed a library book.

Paul Gold

MEDITATION ON - A PLACE WITHIN

Everyone needs a quiet place, a space to go and hide,
but what many of you don't know, you've got one, deep inside.
Whenever you are feeling tired, physically or emotionally drained,
you look at your world in a confused state, you feel very strained.
Don't allow yourself to be torn to shreds or those headaches
                                                    to take hold,
try to find a quiet seat and shelter from the cold.
Once you're feeling comfortable, start to settle down,
allow all those troubles to fade away, lose that worried frown.
Feel the sun above your head, shedding love and light,
let it filter into you, feel its gentle might.
Follow it as it goes inside, watch how deep it drops,
tread gently in its wake, then sit, where'er it stops.
Cultivate this secret place, it's special, just for you.
Sit and wallow in its peace, that's all you have to do.
This place can be a port in storm, for some it's beside the sea,
with a gentle lapping of the waves, a beautiful place to be;
for others it's a waterfall beside a woody glade,
dappled sun shines through the trees to give some welcomed shade.
My place is a garden which brings me so much pleasure,
many memories are stored up there, my little hoard of treasure.
In your little world, you may find birds, or flowers of many kinds;
the beauty is, you can have it all, it's in your fertile minds.
For other souls, their perfect place, is quiet within a room,
with furnishing to suit their taste, an escape from any gloom.
Whatever is your preference, you have it at your feet,
a secret place, a special place, gentle, but oh, so sweet.
Remember, this isn't just for a few, it's there within you all.
Our Father often journeys there, as a result of an anguished call,
so when you're feeling in deep pain, or just to escape life's din!
Gently sit and calm your fears, in that *beautiful place within.*

Beryl Cosgrave

THE HARBOUR

Have you ever stood at the harbour wall,
And stopped to contemplate,
The boats arriving with their haul,
The captain calling his mate.

To stop and watch all the boats,
Heading out to sea.
To watch the way they seem to float,
As further they get from me.

To watch the men come safely in,
After their day of toil.
Weary and tired, but content within,
To come safely into harbour,
As night falls once again.

Then as they trudge home,
They thank the Lord,
For guiding them this day.
They know the perils of the sea,
But know they have to stay.
And they are thankful, just to be,
Safely home this day.

Hilary Ann Torrens

MY ENGLAND

England, a pleasant land to view
In winter harsh or summer dew
The beauty of thy heather moors
Is known far-off on distant shores.

The grandeur of thy stately hills
The pine tree woods and trickling rills
Peaceful pastures where cattle graze
Warm April showers and sunny days.

The fresh sweet smell of bluebell dells
Fine golden sands and ocean swells
November fogs and autumn mists
And orchards ripe with fruit sun-kissed.

What noble deeds for thy dear name
What battles fought that brought us fame
Our hearts will always yearn for thee
England - the land of liberty.

Cynthia Hewer

GARDEN OF TRANQUILLITY

If the sun shines bright tomorrow
I will sit beside my pond
and soak up the sights of nature
because of her I'm rather fond

I'll watch my fishes swimming
in and out among the weed
and listen to the birds that sing
because their song is sweet indeed

I'll take pleasure from the flowers
and their aroma I'll inhale
and enjoy the peace within my garden
which I know will never fail

It never ceases to restore me
when I am feeling low
because the beauty of all nature
gives me such a pleasant glow

I like watching all the butterflies
and bees busy making honey
and the little frogs that hop around -
in fact I find them funny

I'll find the waterfall so restful
that I will close my eyes
and soak up all the scents and sounds
and wake up with a surprise

So please let it be fine tomorrow
then I will lie out in the sun
and communicate with nature
until the day is done

Gill Brion

PRIDE OR PREJUDICE

The cobbled street, it seems quite bare.
I have a little time to sit and stare.
A quiet day, with nowhere to go,
Just watching people, hurry to and fro.
Weeds are growing in the walls,
Buddleia, valerian, in gaps so small.
Nature's way of fighting back,
Plants are growing in every crack.
No-one sees the beauty here,
Spending their lives, living in fear,
Of being mugged, robbed, or worse,
Crime in the world, it is a curse.
Neglected houses, paint it peels.
How does the inhabitant really feel.
Do they not care, or are they poor,
Rubbish is strewn across the floor.
Neglected gardens, broken fence,
I really cannot see the sense.
A pretty street, it could be indeed,
Some loving care, is all it needs.
Surely someone has the skill,
Maybe others have the will,
To make their street a place to smile.
Do the work, then rest a while.
Be proud of their labours, an effort by all,
Community spirit, is the name to call,
Across the rooftops, and into the air.
Not a dream, if people would share.

Jane Rennie

A FAMILIAR PLACE

This house was once full of life
A cosy home a husband and wife
Laughter and fun with daughter and sons
A dog and cat stretched out on a mat
Mrs in the kitchen with the daily chores
Cooking meals for evermore
With oven-baked cakes ready to taste
Spread on the table never no waste
Mr relaxing in his rocking chair
A special place for no one would dare

Now the house stands quiet and still
No cat to sit on the windowsill
Rooms now stand empty and bare
There's just the old rocking chair
Curtains closed to keep out the light
For no one visits this rundown site
The test of time has taken its toll
For the house has finally lost its glow
Familiar voices I hear no more
As I step out and lock the door.

Sonia Coneye

TRAVEL WRITING

Sometimes things seem far away,
The kitchen is a long way from the living-room.
Perhaps I should write a travel book.

How soon a field full of cows,
Becomes a cow full of fields.
None at all,
On the way to my kitchen.

'Fields' that is,
Though it's carpeted.
Not buttercups swaying,
But it has a floral pattern amongst the tea-stains.

Freya Stark never came this way.
She'd have chosen the more difficult route,
Round the edge of the room,
Over shelves and bookcases.

On horseback?
Better for the energy but she may stumble,
Over the wrongly labelled cassette cases.
Best leave the horse in the car-port.

But that's what they all said.
And there's no Tigris to be found in the kitchen.
Just the gentle play of water from taps.
Past no ancient palaces.

Paul Theroux wouldn't like the lack of rails.
Norman Lewis couldn't cope with the meals-on-wheels,
And when he met Freya - *doyen meets doyenne*,
His choice of hat would be crucial.

Not quite a rainforest on the kitchen windowsill,
But you could sweat on hot days,
With no perspiring Attenborough to explain.

Steve Taylor

EARLY MORNING STILLNESS

Still the cool sands,
Crunching barely in the pale, white sun.
Tiny gems from a myriad foreign lands.
A journey begun
In - who knows when or where?
Who knows what magic homeland gave them birth,
Or which mysterious shoreline waved goodbye?
How many aeons washed beneath the waves
Before they came to rest where now they lie?
What stories could they share?
What tales reveal?

Still the cool sands,
And still the quiet air,
Save a faint sound,
Somewhere unfurled,
And almost drowned
By silence.
High, alone,
Releasing there
Its distant, lazy drone.

Still the cool sands, the quiet air,
And still the early sea,
Polished azure in the morning light,
Dusted with brightness
From a reaching glow,
Transformed to whiteness
As on waves below
The sun breathes silver steel.

So still, majestic, vast the waking world.

Verity Gill Malkinson

INFORMATION

We hope you have enjoyed reading this book - and that you will continue to enjoy it in the coming years.

If you like reading and writing poetry drop us a line, or give us a call, and we'll send you a free information pack.

Write to :-
Poetry Now Information
1-2 Wainman Road
Woodston
Peterborough
PE2 7BU
(01733) 230746